© Aladdin Books Ltd

Design: Malcolm Smythe
Text: Kate Petty

ISBN 0 531 04902 7

LCCC No. 84 52508

Separation by La Cromolito, Milan
Typesetting by Dorchester Typesetting
Printed in Belgium

Designed and produced by
Aladdin Books Ltd
70 Old Compton Street
London W1

*First published in
the United States in 1985 by*
Franklin Watts
387 Park Avenue South
New York, NY10016

Contents

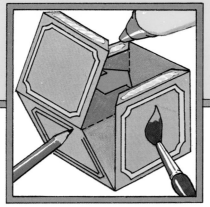

Build Your Own

CASTLE

Consultant Caroline Pitcher

Illustrated by Louise Nevett

Franklin Watts

New York · London · Toronto · Sydney

ABOUT THIS BOOK

The project in this book has been designed so that children can build it unaided, either individually or in groups.

Non-readers can follow the step-by-step pictorial instructions. A black key illustration of the finished project appears on each spread with the unit to be completed colored in red.

The materials for making the project are generally available at home and in classrooms, but alternatives are often suggested. The materials which you could use for making the project are illustrated opposite. It is a good idea to make a habit of collecting all sorts of household bits and pieces (see p.30). Always rinse out bottles and cartons and make sure they have not contained any dangerous liquids such as bleach or disinfectant.

Tracing

When an outline has to be traced, fix tracing paper over the outline. Trace the outline. Turn over the tracing and rub pencil on the back of the pencil line. Tape the tracing, outline upwards, on paper or cardboard and retrace outline.

Cutting

Make sure that the scissors which children use have rounded ends for safety and never give children a sharp knife. The point of a sharp pencil is a safe and effective way of making holes in cardboard.

Paper and Card

These can be distinguished in the instructions by the different colors shown here. Paper is white and card is blue in color. Remember to cut along solid lines and fold along dotted lines.

Glueing

Any sort of ordinary paste or glue is suitable for making the project but very strong glue can be dangerous and should be avoided.

Coloring

For shiny or plastic surfaces use poster paint or powder paint. Ordinary powder paint or watercolor can be used successfully on other surfaces. Alternative coloring methods are wax crayons, colored pencils or felt-tip pens and painting sticks. Large areas can be covered with colored paper. Make sure that the colors you use are lead-free and nontoxic.

WHAT YOU MAY NEED

Scissors

Cork

Scotch tape

Coins

Toothpicks

Rubber bands

Glue

Knitting yarn

Cotton

Modeling clay

Cotton thread spool

Tinfoil

Yogurt or cream container

Paper

Cardboard

Small box

Matchboxes

Used matchsticks

Kitchen knife

Pencil

Paintbrush

Pipe cleaner

Drinking straw

String

Plastic bottle

Quart milk or juice carton

One-pint milk or juice carton

Large cardboard roll

Small cardboard roll

Large box

5

GATEHOUSE AND DRAWBRIDGE

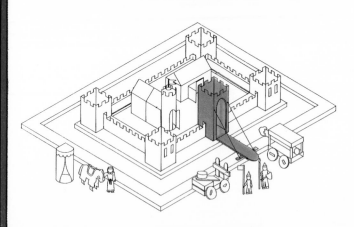

★ A quart milk or juice carton makes the best gatehouse, but any box of similar shape can be used.

★ Take care when you cut out the drawbridge. You must push the scissors through the carton and cut around the line. Remember that the drawbridge is hinged at the bottom.

★ Use the sharp point of a pencil to make holes for the string which will lower and raise the drawbridge.

★ When you have threaded the two pieces of string through the holes, tie knots in each one at the front. With the drawbridge lowered, tie the other ends together at the back. Now you can pull the string to raise the bridge.

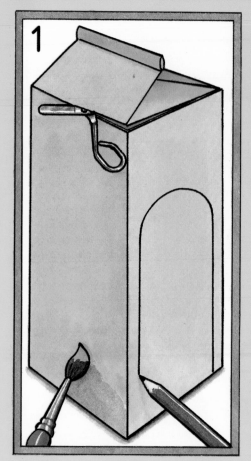

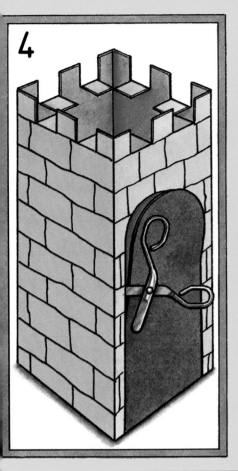

4

5

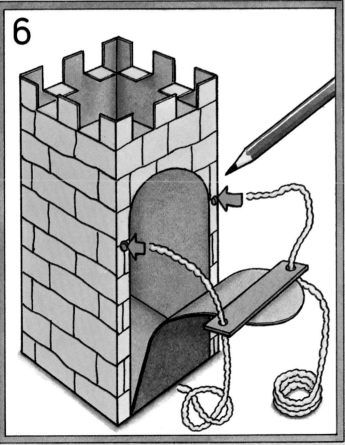

6

7

TOWERS AND BATTLEMENTS

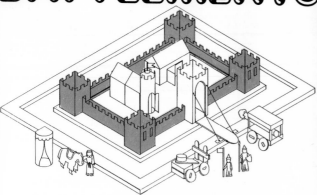

★ You need to make four towers and five battlements. Use one-pint milk or juice cartons for the towers. Any similar boxes will do but they should be shorter than the gatehouse.

★ The length of three of the battlements should be twice the height of the gatehouse. The remaining two battlements will go each side of the gatehouse. Cut them to size when you assemble the castle.

★ The battlements should be as high as the tops of the windows in the towers.

★ A folded piece of card cut to the same length as each battlement and glued on behind makes a platform to stand your people on.

★ Make sure that the whole construction is going to stand square before finally fixing the battlements to the towers.

1

2

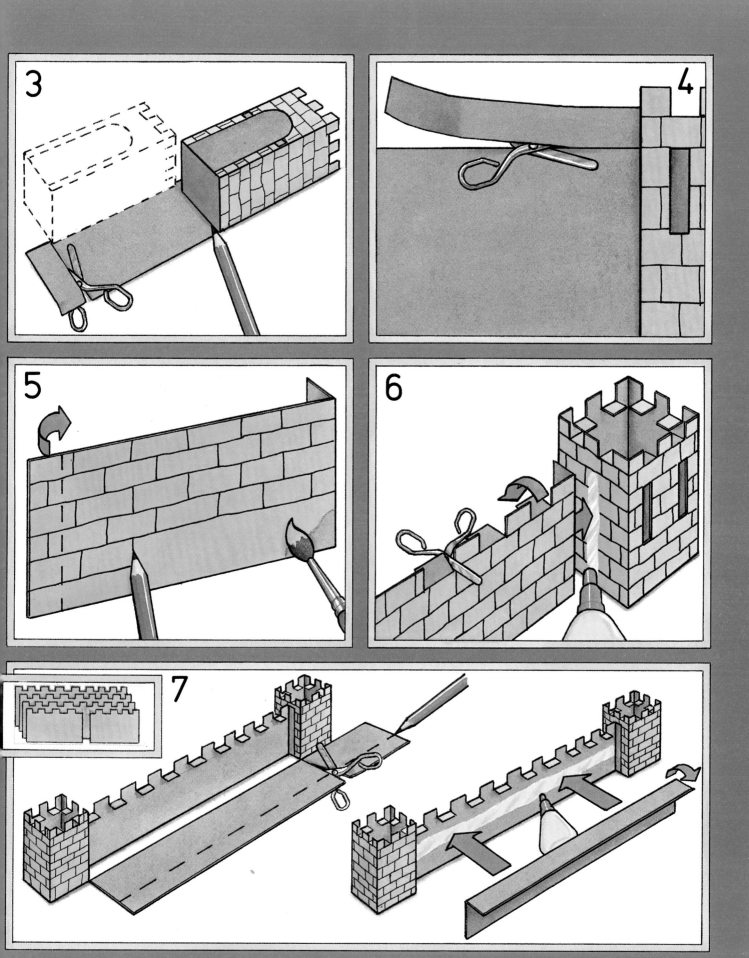

CHURCH

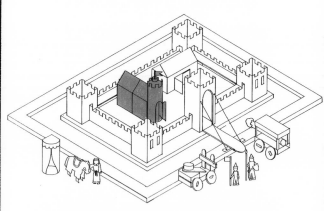

★ Small cartons (one-pint) are ideal for the church because the tops of the cartons are the right shape for the roof. If you use a box instead, make the roof from folded card.

★ Paint the windows to look like colored glass if you want. You can make more elaborate "stained glass" windows from colored paper or tissue.

★ Use a small plastic bottle for the church tower. If you don't have one, use a cardboard tube or a rolled-up sheet of card.

★ When you cut the doors in the church tower, remember that they are hinged at each side.

★ Put modeling clay in the top of the church tower to stick the flag in. If you use a cardboard tube, attach the flag with scotch tape.

★ Use any design you like for the flag.

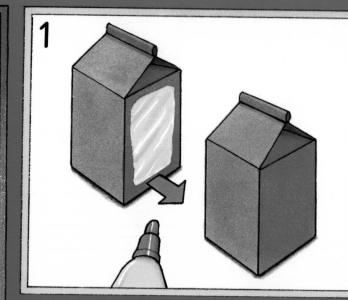

1

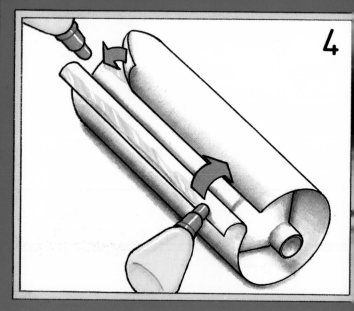

4

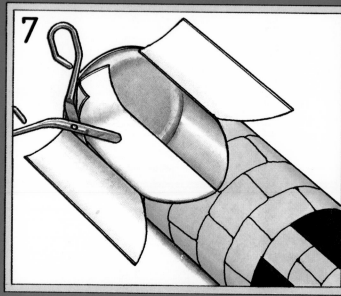

7

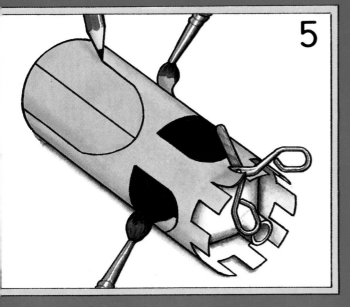

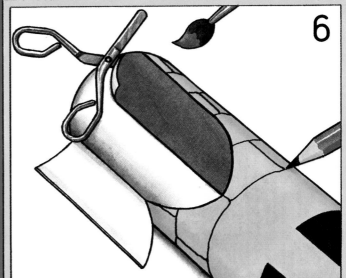

BATTLE TENT AND STABLE

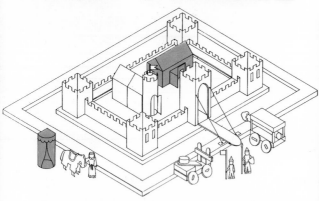

★ Make the tent from a small cardboard tube, or use a rolled and glued sheet of card. Cover it with colored cloth. Patterned paper can be used instead of cloth.

★ The frill which goes around the top of the tent should be a little longer than the cardboard tube.

★ Check, as you are making it, that the cone for the top of the tent will fit correctly.

★ The stable is best made from a child's shoebox, but any similar box will do.

★ The card for the stable roof should be about twice the size of the base of the box. When the roof has been glued in place, cover it with pieces of yellow knitting yarn, or raffia, or even real straw if you can find some.

1

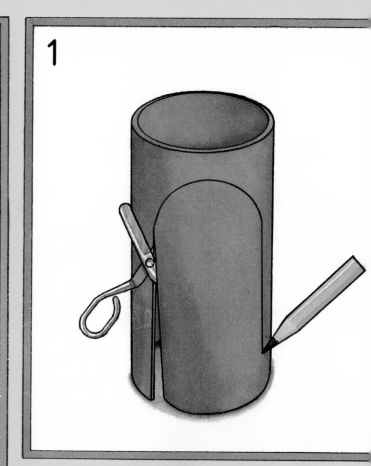

1

2

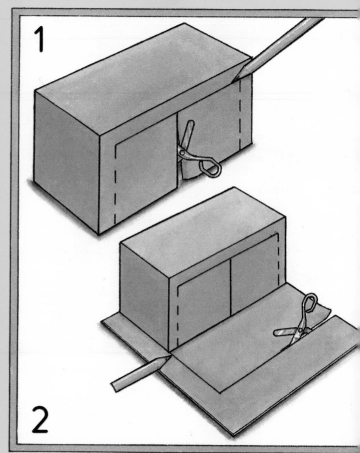

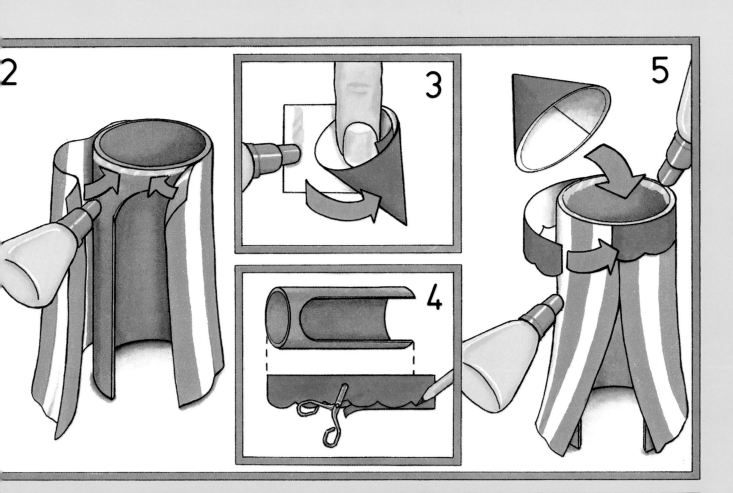

MODEL FOR PEOPLE

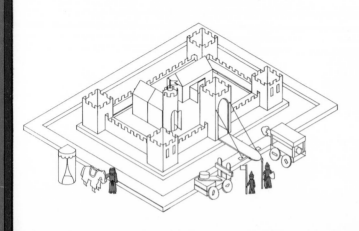

★ Make sure that your people are not too big for the buildings or the horses! Cut up small cardboard tubes or use thick rolled paper for their bodies.

★ Secure the legs in the tube with a lump of modeling clay. Make the feet from a small ball of modeling clay cut in half.

★ Use the sharp point of a pencil to make holes in the body. Push the paper-covered pipe cleaner arms through the holes, bend and cut to size.

★ Mold the head very carefully from modeling clay. The people will wear hats when you dress them so there is no need to make hair.

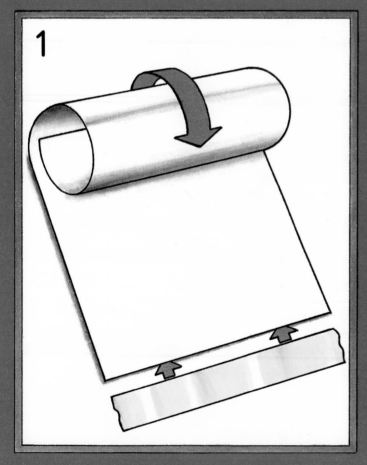

1

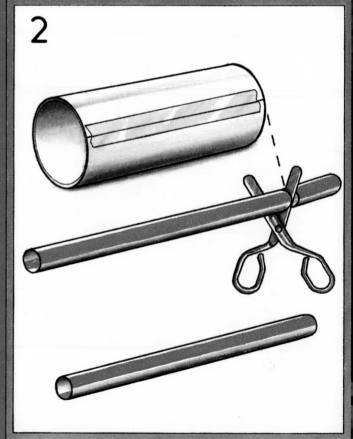

2

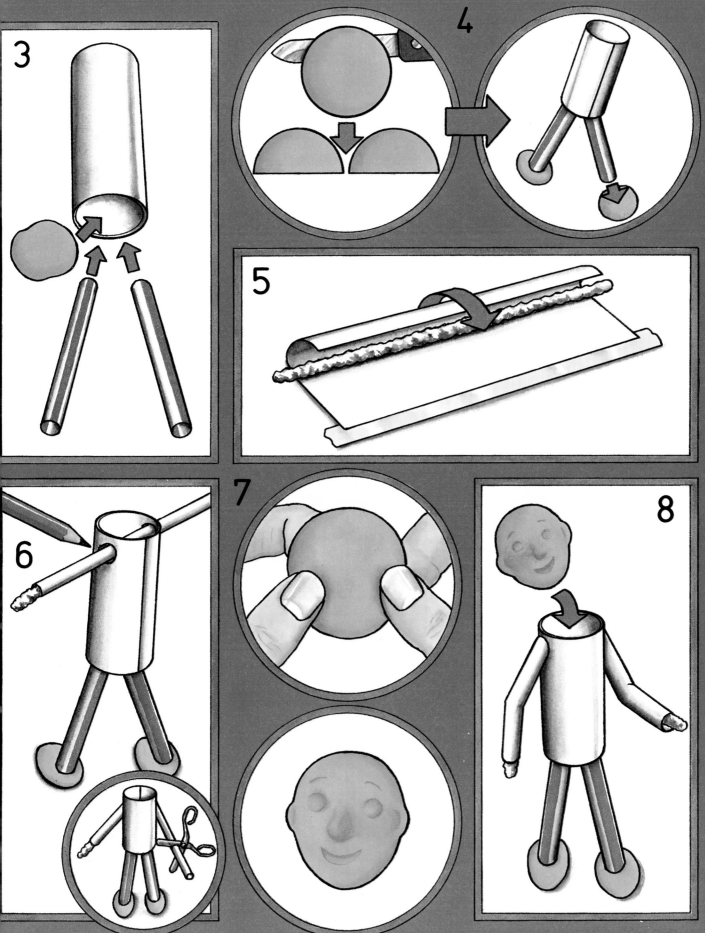

3

4

5

6

7

8

KNIGHT AND LADY

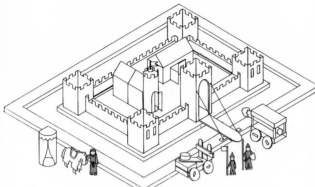

★ Make sure each hat is going to fit its wearer before you carry on making it.

★ Glue a piece of cloth over the circle of card for the lady's head-dress.

★ Make a cone of card to fit the circle for the knight's helmet.

★ You could try making tall, pointed cones for some of the ladies' hats, or make them braids from yarn for hair.

★ Make the lady's dress from a folded piece of cloth with a slit cut for her head. Cut a dress shape and decorate with cotton, lace or sequins.

★ You can make chain mail from tinfoil dotted with a pencil. Make the knight's robe from a piece of cloth, colored paper or tissues.

★ The frill that goes around the top of the tent should be a little longer than the cardboard tube.

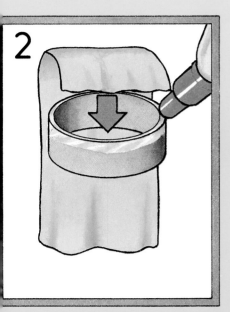

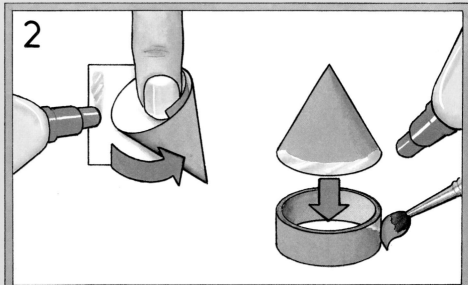

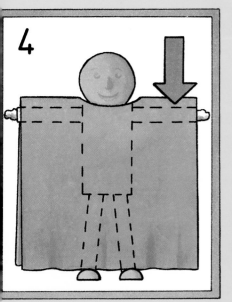

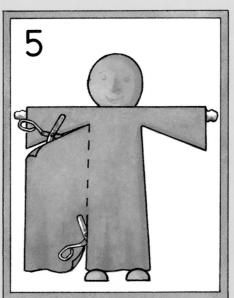

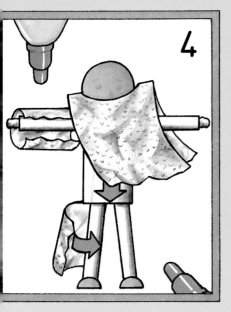

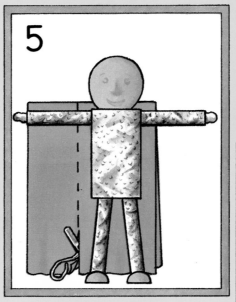

19

LANCES, PENNANTS, SHIELDS AND SWORD

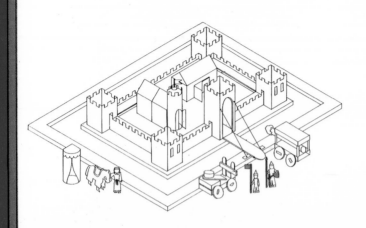

★ Copy the shapes for the lances from picture 1. Paint them before you cut them out. Make slots in the straws and secure the heads in place with scotch tape.

★ Make the pennants and shields from thin card. Vary the shape and design. Make sure that armies fighting against each other have different designs!

★ Use a piece of ribbon for the strap on the sword and attach it with scotch tape. Make the scabbard from colored paper or you can use tinfoil instead.

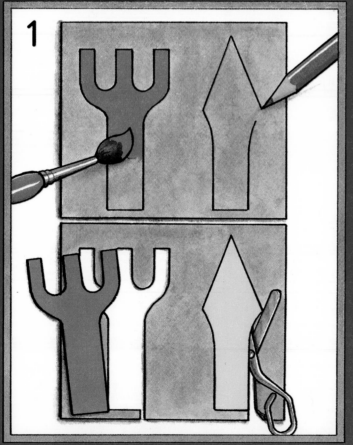

1

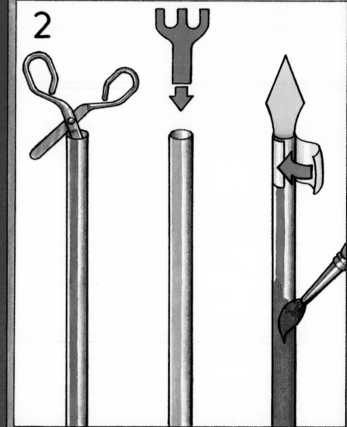

2

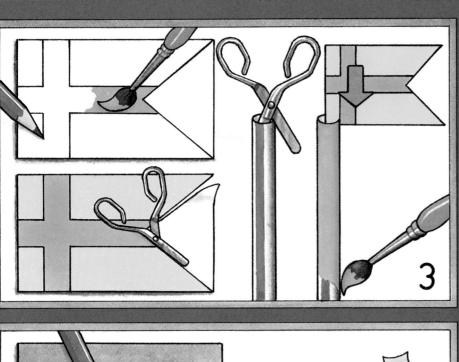

3

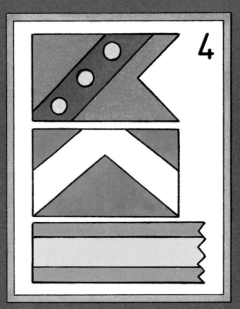

4

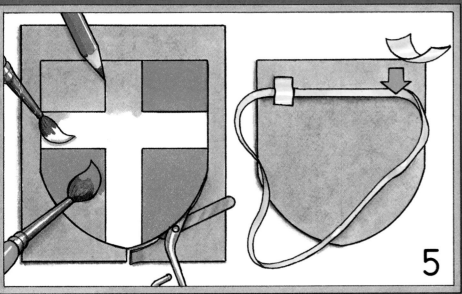

5

6

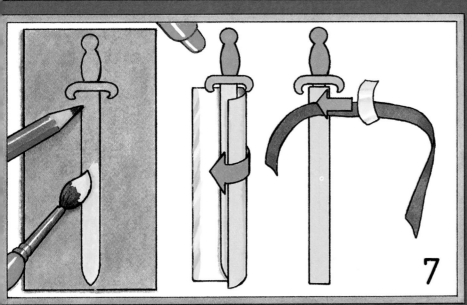

7

8

21

HORSES

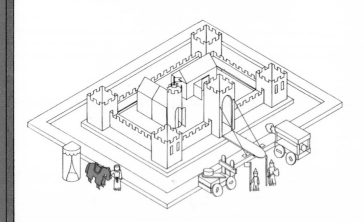

★ Use stiff card to make the horses. Trace the outline in picture 1 onto the folded card. Position it as shown, so that the dotted lines are along the fold. Be sure not to cut along the dotted lines.

★ Paint the horses and saddles and then decorate their robes with bright colors.

★ You could glue cloth or patterned paper cut to size onto the horses' robes, and make their tails from pieces of knitting yarn glued into position.

★ See if your knights will fit on the horses' backs and secure them in the saddle with modeling clay.

1

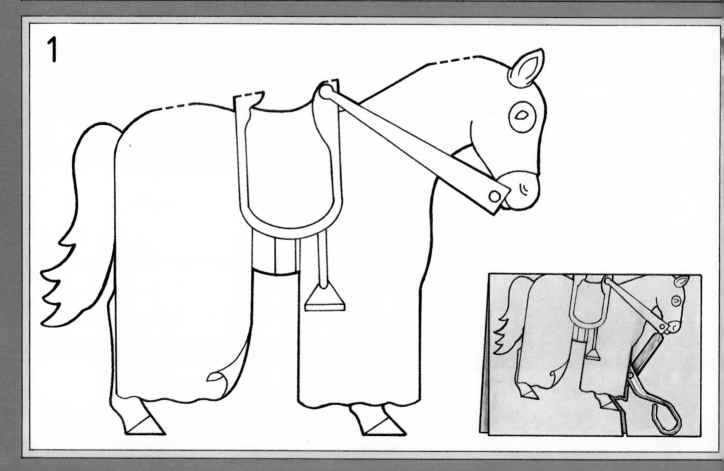

BATTERING RAM

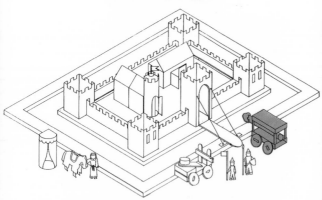

★ A large matchbox is best for this, but any box of a similar shape will do. If using a matchbox, the tray forms the roof and the outside becomes the base of the battering ram. If you don't use a matchbox you can make the roof from a piece of card.

★ Measure the four straws for the corners against the width of the box and fix them in position with modeling clay.

★ Turn the battering ram on its roof to attach the straw axles. Make the wheels from stiff card. They will turn if you attach them with pipe cleaners threaded through the straws. Make the holes in the wheels with a sharp pencil.

★ You can make a simpler model by glueing the wheels right onto the matchbox.

★ Fix modeling clay onto the pointed end of the pencil and your battering ram is ready for action.

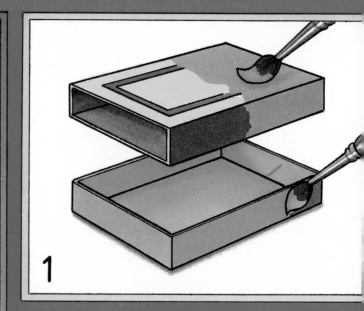

1

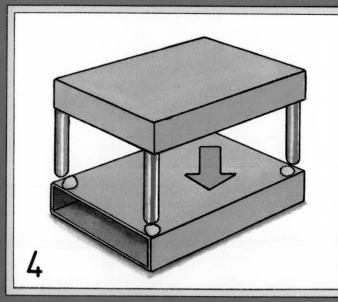

4

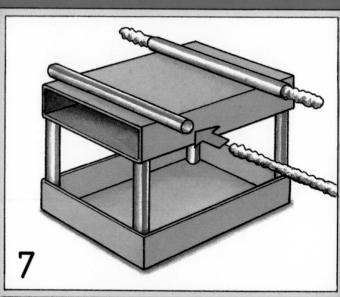

7

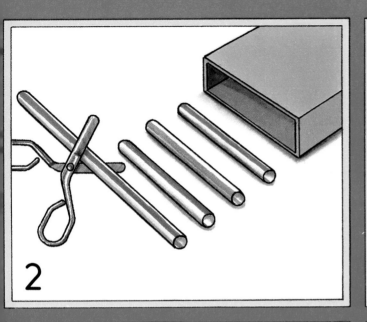

2

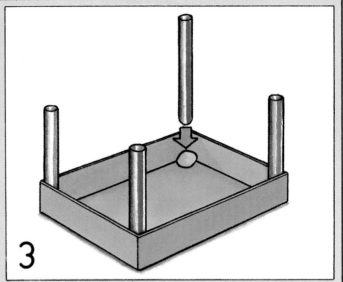

3

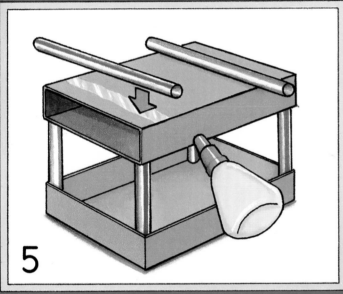

5

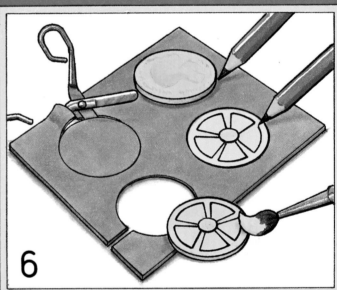

6

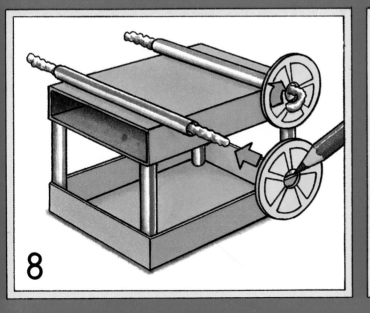

8

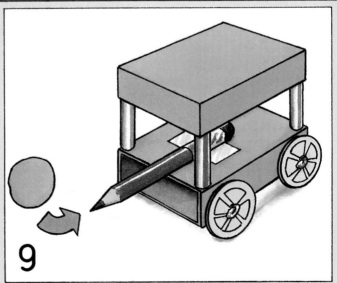

9

CATAPULT

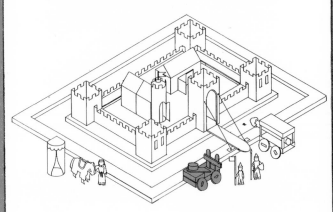

★ This is made from a large matchbox, but a smaller one will do. Make a slot for the popsicle stick about one third of the way along the tray.

★ Use a sharp pencil to make the hole for the rubber band. Loop both ends around the popsicle stick and wind until the rubber band is taut.

★ Glue a small matchbox tray at the back of the catapult for storing ammunition.

★ Before you break the popsicle stick for the barrier, score across it with the scissors. Bend it backward and forward until it snaps.

★ Make the wheels from thick card. They will turn if you thread pipe cleaners through the straws. Make holes in the wheels with a sharp pencil. You can make a simpler model by glueing the wheels right onto the box.

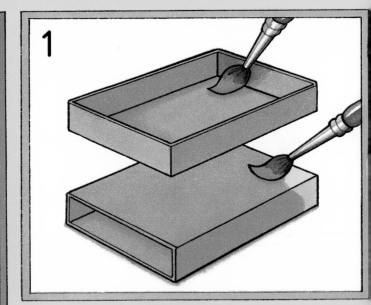

1

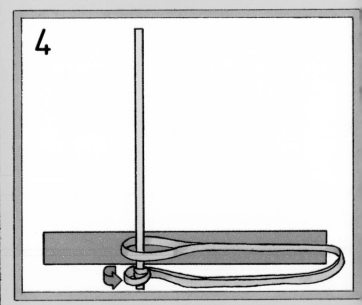

4

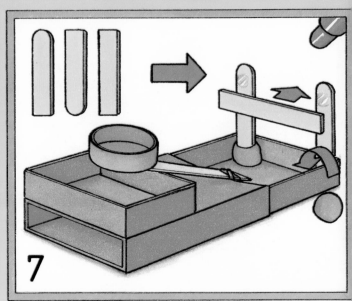

7

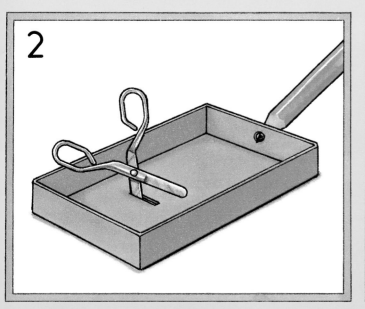

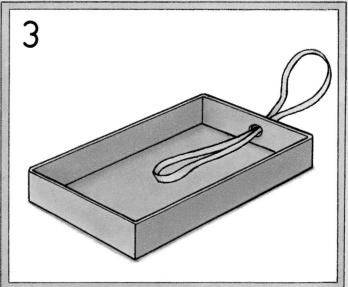

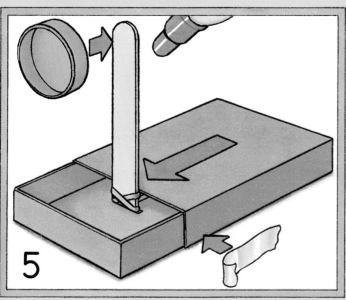

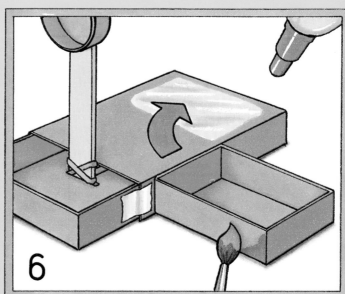

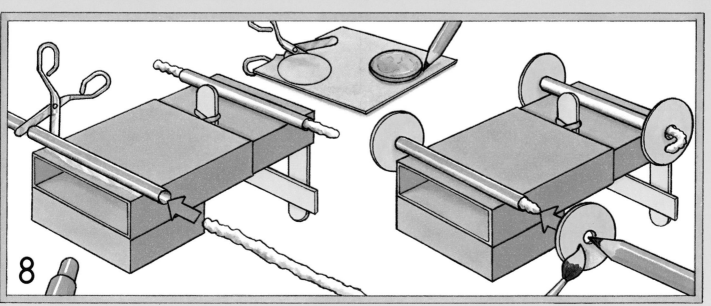

CASTLE BASE AND MOAT

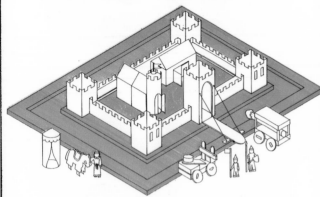

★ You need a large square of thick board to make the base.

★ The base is built up from papier mâché. Make this by soaking a lot of torn-up newspaper in flour and water paste. While it is soaking, mark where the castle will stand on the base. Leave room for the moat and for the slopes all around.

★ Press the wet papier mâché onto the board. Build up the mound for the castle to stand on as shown. Make the moat by pressing a ruler into the papier mâché before it dries.

★ The base will be ready to paint in around six hours.

★ Place the finished castle on a table which has been covered with cloth or paper. Arrange your knights, ladies, horses, catapults, battering rams and battle tents around and about.

1

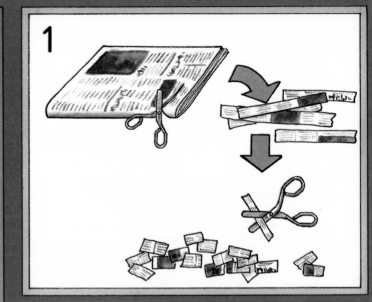

2

3

4

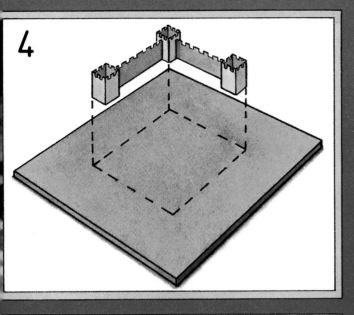

5

6

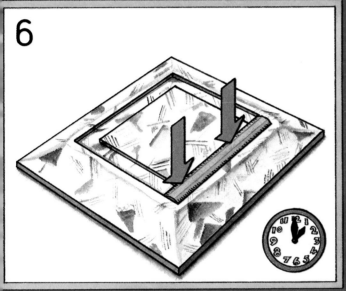

7

8

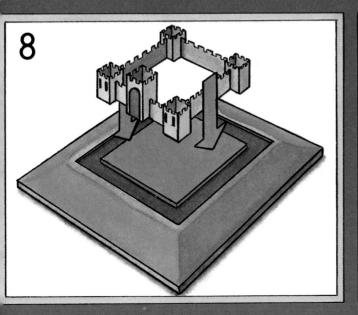

9

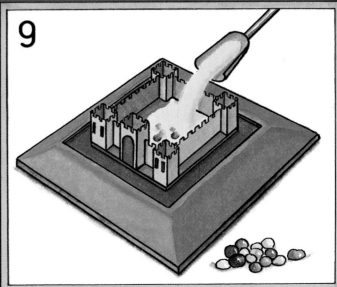

BITS BOX

Collect all sorts of household bits and pieces on a regular basis.
They can provide an endless source of creative play for children, not
only for making the projects in this book but also enabling children
to invent models of their own. Keep everything together in a "bits box."

PRINTED IN BELGIUM BY

proost

INTERNATIONAL BOOK PRODUCTION